A HANDBOOK FOR WIDOWS

by

Corrine Jacobson

and

Rose M. Rubin

A Handbook For Widows

Printed in the United States of America

C. A. Bond, Publisher
5845B Westhaven Dr.
Fort Worth, TX 76132
Contact at: 817-294-7844

Library of Congress Cataloging-in-Publication Data
Jacobson, Corrine and Rubin, Rose M.

A Handbook for Widows

ISBN 978-0-615-26424-0

Library of Congress Control Number: ***

PREFACE

Corrine Jacobson and her husband, Phil, were both healthy 66-year-olds, packing for a trip to Seattle and Lake Tahoe, when he died unexpectedly. Instead of boarding an airplane, in a matter of days, Corrine was seated in a hearse en route to the cemetery.

During the first 48 hours following her husband's death, Corrine had gathered her children and stepchildren from cities around the country and summoned one relative home from France. Unfortunately, her rabbi was out of town, so a clergyman she did not know very well officiated at the funeral. Her friends brought platters of food to her home, although Corrine had no appetite.

After 22 years of marriage, all of a sudden, without preparation, Corrine had to embark on a new life. How to proceed? Frankly, it was by trial and error. "Nobody told me what to do," she recalled. She was faced with an obituary to write, medical bills to pay, insurance policies to read, an estate to settle, and legal procedures to deal with. During her career as a businesswoman, Corrine had run a $7 million-a-year company; she had raised two children and three stepchildren; she had been a Sunday school superintendent and a community volunteer. None of those experiences had prepared her for the road ahead.

Fortunately, Corrine is an organized person with an administrative and managerial background. She began creating file folders for each task that lay before her and for each professional she was advised to contact—from stockbrokers to Social Security administrators. Corrine's close friend, Dr. Rose M. Rubin, observed how methodically Corrine went about each task. She also noted how cathartic it was for Corrine to handle the estate herself. Rose, who is an economics professor and published writer, suggested they collaborate on a manual to be titled, A *Handbook for Widows,* a book that would help anyone who lost a spouse.

If you are reading this manual, then you are likely to be a widow—or perhaps a widower. You need to realize this is a condition that cannot be reversed. Facing reality is your first step. What do you do? How do you handle this new and different status? We all need practical advice. This book presents you with practical, positive, and constructive ways to handle yourself at this difficult time. This manual will aid you in finding the help you now need to make new decisions and to face the enormous task of developing a new lifestyle.

It is Corrine and Rose's belief that by living your own life in a positive and constructive way, you will gradually work through the many challenges of your spouse's death in the manner best suited to yourself. After reading this book, you won't encounter as many surprises or roadblocks in the months after your spouse has passed away. You won't have to figure out everything as you go along. This book can become your guide.

A HANDBOOK FOR WIDOWS
CONTENTS

THE IMMEDIATE THINGS – A QUICK CHECK LIST

This check list presents a brief listing of the things that will have to be done in the first difficult hours or day following the loss of your loved one. Each of these is detailed in the first chapter, but this list offers an easy quick reference.

Remember that others will want to help you at this time, and you can delegate a great many tasks. Do not hesitate to let family and friends know what they can actually do to help you the most with large or small tasks.

Notifying family and friends

- Your children and close family members and friends must be informed right away so that you can comfort each other and make necessary plans.

- You will need to notify your minister or rabbi or priest immediately for comfort and to plan the date and time of the funeral so that this information is available for calling people and for the obituary.

- For those coming from out of town, be certain someone is in charge of meeting planes or arranging places to stay.

Plan the Funeral

- This is the time that preplanned funeral arrangements show their value, and you will be greatly relieved to know you have done much of this in advance.

- Otherwise, there are immediate decisions to make. Seek any advice and counsel that will help you.

- Make a list of what you want for the funeral processes and services; and include any preferences your spouse may have expressed or that your children may have.

- Meet with your spiritual leader as soon as possible to make the funeral arrangements and discuss your preferences in detail.

- Do not hesitate to ask about costs and to get all costs itemized from the mortuary.

- When you go to the funeral home, remember take the clothing you want your spouse to be buried in.

The Obituary

- The obituary should contain all the necessary details about the funeral and/or viewing. This will also serve to inform local persons about the death and funeral.

- Try to think of the important details of your spouse's life that you want noted.

- Be certain to list all the close family members in the obituary.

Prepare yourself for the funeral

- You will have to force yourself to face this day and to get through it to the very best of your ability.

- You should lean on others and ask for help with anything, large or small. Let others do what they can to help you or do what has to be done.

- Remember to arrange for someone to be at the house during the funeral.

SECTION ONE

FIRST THINGS FIRST

The fear that I would
come home one day and
find you gone has turned
into the pain of the reality.
"What will I do if it happens?"
I would ask myself.
What will I do now that it has?

Peter McWilliams
How to Survive the Loss of a Love, page 11

It's a Difficult Time

It will take real and conscious efforts on your part to get through the first few hours and days of widowhood, and then to rediscover and redefine your own everyday life. Decisions that will shape the balance of your life will now be made by you alone, no matter how much discussion and help you seek. You will survive, you will be strong, and you will move forward and establish your own life. But recognize that this will not be easy.

You may now feel lost, but do not look at life as emptiness forever. Decide what you can handle during these first days of widowhood, whether that means being alone or being with selected friends and relatives. Do what suits you. During the initial days, do not worry about anyone else. Do not handle more than is possible for you; you are the only one who knows what you can cope with.

Notifying Family and Friends

One of the most difficult tasks you immediately face is the need to notify family, friends, co-workers, and acquaintances that your spouse has passed away. You or the attending doctor or your spiritual leader will tell your children as soon as possible. You may also want the help of your minister or rabbi or doctor in telling some other relatives.

This task of sharing the sad news of your spouse's death may seem insurmountable; however, promptly notifying relatives, friends, business associates, and others is important. They will want to be informed, but other people besides you may be able to make many of the actual calls from your list. This sad task can be divided among your children, yourself, and other relatives, and friends. You might call some family members or close friends and ask them to be in charge of informing groups of people, or one person might do all of this calling for you. If you have an up-to- date address and telephone list, it will be easier to arrange for others to make calls. No matter how hard it is to concentrate at this time, make the effort to be certain that everyone in your circles of family, friends, and business associates is notified.

Before telephoning others, especially out-of-towners, gather and write down as much information as possible about the funeral, including the name, phone number, and Internet address of the funeral home, so that these calls do not have to be repeated. If you have not yet arranged the time of a service, ask people to call you or your family back, or to contact the funeral home, or to check online, so you do not have to keep phoning each other.

The newspaper obituary, which generally is posted on the Internet, will become a major source of informing people, especially locally. This will save you a lot of time and phone calls. In the obituary, include all the necessary information about the funeral service, the viewing, and any preferences about memorial donations. If relatives or friends are traveling to the funeral from out of town, remember that some airlines may provide bereavement fares for those making expensive last-minute reservations. To qualify for a discount, passengers must be immediate family and generally listed in the obituary.

Assign specific family members or friends the task of meeting relatives at the airport, or have the airport-shuttle schedule on hand when relatives are called. Also, delegate to someone the hostess role of making certain that those arriving from out of town will have a place to stay.

Later, to contact more distant friends and acquaintances, you can go through your and your spouse's address books and write or call these people to advise them of the death. People care and will want to respond to you if they are informed. Relatives or friends who offer to help you may be willing to write some of these letters. This will give them something useful to do when they really do want to be helpful.

Planning the Funeral

If you have made preplanned funeral arrangements, you will now recognize how fortunate you were to plan ahead. You will quickly see how much this relieves a major strain immediately after confronting the loss of your spouse.

Whether you have preplanned or not, you will need to meet with your spiritual leader as soon as possible to make the funeral arrangements. You may call the final arrangements anything you want, e.g. a "memorial service" or a "graveside service." But there is no soft word or phrase that will lessen the blow of your spouse's death at this moment. Compose yourself to the best of your ability, as the hardest time of your life is here. You must plan the funeral of your mate.

Before your spiritual leader arrives, meet with your family and have them write down what you feel, and perhaps what they, too, feel and recall. This will ease the discussion. Jot down a list of what you want to discuss about the funeral and any preferences your spouse may have expressed. It may easier to have your children read what you want in the way of a funeral and eulogy, than to say the words yourself. Again, lean on your family; they want to help you.

The Eulogy. Have the family help you remember anything that you want said in the eulogy or that they may wish to add. No matter how well your mate did or did not know your rabbi, priest or minister, the family knows the moments that meant the most. This is a good time to ask children, siblings, or close friends if they wish to say a few words or read something at the service. Grandchildren, children, or friends may want to speak or have a message read. In planning the service, it is a good idea to include any tribute that helps you and members of your family think positively about the life of your loved one.

Compose yourself to the best of your ability and try to think what should be included at the funeral. This event may feel like it is happening to someone else, but it is you and your life. If you have been fortunate enough to make funeral plans in advance, you will be spared some of this extra grief. Most of us do not plan funerals ahead, so you will have to see that everything is the way you and your closest family want it. Remember that the purpose of the funeral is to help the family get through these trying days.

For Veterans. If your spouse was a veteran, special burial arrangements and services are available. Call a friend connected with the military and also call the nearest Veterans Administration office to get detailed information. This may vary from place to place and for different branches of the military.

The Funeral Home. Before your first visit to the funeral home, estimate what you can afford. Remember the price the funeral director quotes you usually does not include burial and cemetery expenses or the cost of publishing the obituary. Be sure to get all itemized costs from the mortuary. It may be difficult, but it is very important that you insist on an itemized statement and go over it carefully. Perhaps you will ask an adult child or other close relative or friend to look at this with you.

When you go to the funeral home, take the clothing that you want your husband to wear in his casket. You might decide what you want, then ask your family to find these garments in his closet and drawers. You might choose his best clothing or his college sweater. How you remember him enjoying life is a good way to select what he will wear in death.

The funeral should be what you and your immediate family want. It might be of comfort to include a favorite photo, birthday card, letter, or a family portrait in the casket. You must think about this now, no matter how hard it is. Try to have everything the way you want. You do not have a second funeral, thank goodness, so try your best to have this one the way you want.

Your religion may have traditional music or prayers at this time. Seek what comforts you, even if it may seem unconventional to others. If your favorite song is part of your life, play a CD; or if he loved a certain symphony, use this as background. Or you may prefer to have a family member or friend sing at the service. Make it easiest and most suitable for yourself. Some families like to develop a "memory board" to view at the funeral home. This might be a collage of pictures depicting the life of your loved one. Your children or other relatives might find this a comforting memorial to compile for you.

Although it is especially difficult to think of practical matters at this time, try to compose your thoughts before you visit the funeral home. Before you go, estimate what you can afford. You may want to discuss this with your children or other family members. Be certain that whoever is making the funeral arrangements for you or with you gets all the details and financial information in writing, so that no misunderstandings occur. Review these plans carefully to make certain everything is acceptable and affordable.

Be sure to get all of the costs in writing from the mortuary. There may be numerous things that come with a funeral package and others that are itemized or additional. Whoever is doing this will need to ask a lot of questions and should feel comfortable asking about everything until all the details are clear. Also note that there will be choices available in planning the funeral and that these are not always spelled out in detail. Often, families are too upset to catch all the details the first time they are mentioned. Do not hesitate to ask questions and to question the cost of each item. You do not want any unexpected charges showing up later. Note that the price quoted by the funeral home usually does not include cemetery expenses or the cost of publishing the obituary.

There may be alternative options and possibilities to consider. If you or members of the family prefer to hire transportation separately, a rented limousine service may be much less costly than the funeral home limos. If you and members of the family are using family cars, ask a friend to have them washed today.

Someone at Your Home. One other thing to note in planning the funeral: Have someone stay at your home during the funeral to answer the phone and prevent a potential burglary. Unfortunately, this is a necessary security measure, because potential intruders will have read the newspaper obituary page and may assume that the house will be vacant during the funeral. You might ask a neighbor or an employee who does not feel it necessary to attend the funeral to stay at your house.

Keep a List. It is a good idea to set out a notebook or sheets of paper for listing people who telephone their condolences, visit, or bring food to your house. Later you will want to thank everyone for his or her thoughtfulness. You might put one or two family members or friends in charge of the list. Also, be certain there is a sign-in book at the funeral. This may be provided by the funeral home, but if not, delegate this to a family member or friend who can also remind people to sign. You are unlikely to note or recall everyone who attended, and will want to refer back to this later.

The Obituary

Think about the newspaper obituary before you go to the funeral home. If you can manage to give this some thought, it will be easier to have it written the way you want it. Your mind is in a haze, and you wonder whether this can be you, writing facts about your partner's life. It is, therefore, important to have the following information for both your mortuary and religious leader:

1. Spouse's full name

2. Date of birth and birthplace

3. Education

4. Marriage date

5. Names of survivors and the cities where they reside. List children, stepchildren, grandchildren, step-grandchildren, brothers, and sisters.

6. Organizations of which he was a member or volunteer. This can include fraternities, religious organizations, professional groups, and hobby organizations.

7. If you want donations made to your congregation or favorite charity, be sure the newspaper includes the appropriate address so people will know where to send their thoughtful contribution. This is often the last part of the newspaper obituary.

Ask the newspaper or funeral home to call and read you the obituary, or to e-mail it to you *before it is published*. Be certain it says what you want. Sometimes, the newspaper condenses the obituary, and the family's most important memory may be deleted. After the obituary is published, you can send copies to your church, college and professional or other publications. This will keep you from having to rewrite notices.

Find the photo, if you want one printed with the obituary. Take this to the funeral home. They will relay it to the newspaper. Some newspapers may charge extra when a photo is included in the obituary or when you have any sort of special listing. Even though it is hard to think to do so, you should feel free to ask about such charges and to find out what is available.

Prepare Yourself for the Funeral

This will be one of the most difficult days you will ever encounter, but you will get through it. You will also find that family members, friends, and others will reach out to try to help you, even though they are also grieving. You will have to force yourself to face this day and this time and to get through it to the very best of your ability. It is all right to lean on others, to cry, to show emotion, and to ask for help with anything, large or small. Let others do what they can to help you or to do what has to be done.

Whenever and wherever possible, take a close relative or friend with you if you have appointments and errands to run. This is not yet the time to go it alone.

If it is important to you to look as well as possible, remember to make, or have someone else, call and make an appointment to have your hair done today or the day of the funeral. Most beauty shops will try to accommodate you under the circumstances and will show respect for your feelings while you are there.

If you like massages, get a massage. This may sound like an indulgence at this time of your life, but you need to make the effort to do something soothing just for yourself. Leave your house with the visitors and family and have a friend take you to the masseuse. Do not drive yourself. If your funds are limited call a "Y" or any salon and explain you have lost your spouse, and you have a trying few days, could they give you a reduced rate? You will be surprised at how people will help you if you ask at this time. An hour of quiet at the masseuse, with soft background music, will give you time to pull yourself together for the funeral.

Following the Funeral

Decide where the family will receive friends after the funeral and burial. This is customary, because people have traveled from out of town to lend emotional support to one another at this delicate time. There is a need to visit, to reminisce, and to convey condolences in person. Therefore, at the close of the funeral service, be certain that the person officiating or a member of the family announces where people will be reconvening. Be certain the address is noted. Advise the person who is staying at the house about these arrangements and anything he or she may need to do to help prepare the house in advance. This is also a good time to let friends who want to help in some way assist with the food, serving, and clean up.

Often, people find it difficult to find the right words for someone who has suffered the loss of a loved one. Some comments may strike you as hurtful rather than helpful. It will, however, almost always be the case that they are trying to be supportive, but they may feel awkward or inadequate expressing their feelings. If you can possibly overlook any awkwardness or perceived slights, your day will go better.

SECTION TWO

YOUR NEXT STEPS

You're a survivor
with all the loneliness
of survivorship.

Joanne Seltzer,
from the poem "The Orphan"
When I am an Old Woman I Shall Wear Purple, page 63

Getting through Each Day and Night

The children have left, your friends cannot come by each night forever, and you have your first evening alone at home. Have a plan for entertaining yourself, or this night will never end. This is a good time to treat yourself and call for food delivery. If you are in a town or city of any size, there is sure to be some sort of "take-out" service available. If you like pizza, Chinese, or Italian food, almost any type of meal can be delivered to your house. Select a movie from the evening's TV listings or rent a DVD. Set up a nice table, burn a little candle, make the setting as relaxed as you can. Enjoy your meal and the movie. Don't spend this first night alone without some agenda for getting through the evening.

Going to bed at night is very difficult. Turn your sheets back early in the evening and it will be easier to get under the covers later. You might try sleeping on his side of the bed or in the middle, so you won't feel the loneliness so badly.

While getting into bed can be traumatic, unfortunately, getting up in the morning can be even harder to face. If you have children or other family living with you, you might be forced to get up and start the day because someone is waiting for you to make breakfast, share a cup of coffee, or drive them to school. If you have to return to work, at least you know that you have a destination that forces you to put one foot in front of the other. If you are alone and are not employed, you may have the choice of doing whatever you want. If so, getting out of bed will require a degree of discipline to motivate yourself to face the day. This might be a good time to schedule volunteer activity so that you have a place to go and a task to perform. Or you might indulge yourself - make a breakfast tray, put a flower on it and go back to bed. Enjoy the morning TV shows or the newspaper or a book and a good breakfast, and then maybe the day will be brighter.

This is also a time in your life when you should talk with other people who have been in your situation. Friends who have been widowed or a support group may have helpful advice and suggestions for you. Ask widows or widowers you know and admire what helped them the most to get through the difficult weeks following their spouses' funerals.

Hold on to Your Memories

Memory is more indelible than ink.

Anita Loos,
The Quotable Woman, page 147

Hold on to your memories of happy times with your spouse. However, you will also need to build new memories. Make some changes in your life that will give you fresh experiences and new memories, along with the old ones, especially at holiday times. They say that time heals most wounds, but actually your mind is the healer. If you think about too many old memories, year in and year out, this may prevent time from being a healer. Make new memories that will ease the indelible old ones.

You will receive many cards, letters, and notices of donations in memory of your spouse. Keep all these cards, letters, and papers in a pretty basket or container or box. Be certain to make a list as each item arrives, so that nothing can get lost or overlooked. You might choose to delegate this task and have someone who is with you at the house relieve you of this. Later, if you wish, you can make a scrapbook of the remembrances from people, articles from the paper, and other memorabilia. This will be meaningful to you and also to your children and grandchildren and help each of you realize the extent that their father or grandfather touched other people's lives.

Think about Your Attitude

Living the past is a dull and lonely business;
looking back strains the neck muscles,

and causes you to bump into people
not going your way.

Edna Ferber,
The Quotable Woman, page 150

Your everyday attitude can be thought of as a scale, like that on a thermometer. Of course you want to be at the optimum healthy temperature (attitude) as much as possible, but for now you may not reach that goal. The trauma of losing a spouse can initiate a roller coaster of emotions and very real depression. Maybe even before your spouse's death your emotions were not at the best level, perhaps due to his illness. Eventually, however, you need to re-store your emotional temperature as close as possible to a "normal" range. Watch yourself, take stock of your emotions, and if you feel that you are too low for more than a few days, seek professional help. Feeling low may be tolerable for a short while, but it is important to recognize when you might need help to cope with the emotional roller coaster of your loss.

Remember in choosing friends that you need to be around positive-thinking people. Negative people will pull you down mentally. Don't keep reminding your friends how sad and lonely you are. When you meet people during the day who say, "how are you," be truthful; tell them this is a sad day. You have recently lost your spouse and you appreciate their caring by asking how you are. If they say, "have a good day," tell them you will try to have a good day at their suggestion, but it is hard. This can make a positive statement for all, and lets you air your sadness.

Discipline

Webster's dictionary defines discipline as "training that develops self control to enforce obedience." At the time of your life when discipline is very hard, you will need to train yourself and your mind to accept your new circumstances. Remember, this is another life for you. You have no spouse to review your situations or problems, and no one to care for you in the middle of the night if you are ill. This is why you will need discipline in your life to handle your affairs, from eating correctly and sleeping, to handling the enormous strains put upon you both physically and mentally. Learn to discipline your mind to handle your new situation. Don't expect it to be easy. It may be easier if you take two or three hours at a time and focus on one task at hand; and do not try to look too far ahead. It is too early to make long range plans for anything that can reasonably be postponed for a while.

Should you visit your spouse's grave? Going to the cemetery is a very individual thing. I went to the cemetery often, as it helped me realize my husband was deceased. He was not going to walk in the door. He was not coming back. The cemetery brought me to reality. Taking fresh flowers and watching the grass around his grave grow back, eased my tensions. This may not be the appropriate route for you, or your religion may not handle death in this manner. Nonetheless, do not let anyone make you feel guilty for visiting, or not visiting, the cemetery. If this helps you emotionally, that is what matters most at this time.

You may find your mind wandering and your concentration not the best, so be especially careful of the following:

1. Don't leave your keys in the car, as it is so easy to forget and lock yourself out of the car.

2. Watch the speed limits when driving, as your mind is apt to wander.

3. When cooking, watch your pots and pans so that you don't forget you have something cooking on the stove or in the oven. Set the kitchen timer.

4. When you leave the house, be sure the keys are in your pocket or purse or in your hand, as locking yourself out of your house is easy to do at this time.

5. If you start anything, remember to finish the task. For example, if you are watering the lawn, remember to move the sprinkler or turn off the system.

Overall, it is important to focus on what you are doing so that other thoughts creeping into your mind do not distract you.

SECTION THREE
HANDLING THE ESTATE

Your motto should be: "Real happiness is found not in doing the things you like to do, but in liking the things you have to do."

Author unknown

You Need to Know and to Notify

There are a several priority items that you should handle without delay to give you greater financial peace of mind.

Bank Accounts. While laws may vary from state to state, you ought to close savings and checking accounts that are in your spouse's name before they are frozen, pending settlement of his estate. Remove important papers from your safe deposit box before it is sealed. Do this before the obituary notice is published in the newspaper, because that is generally how financial institutions learn of a client's death.

Death Certificates. You will need numerous *certified* death certificates and also *copies* of the death certificate for different purposes of settling the estate, insurance, and other needs. A *certified* death certificate is a special copy of the original that is notarized with a seal to guarantee that this is identical to the original legal document. The funeral home generally provides certified copies and may impose a charge for each one. Be certain to order more than you think you may need from the start, as you have to wait to obtain them later, and this will slow up the process of completing the estate transfer to you. Most insurance companies, brokerages, and financial institutions require that you provide a certified copy for their transfer processes. Copies that do not need to be certified can simply be made at any copy machine. It will be easier if you have these on hand as you need them.

Social Security. If your spouse was receiving Social Security payments, you will need to notify the Social Security Administration, which probably will require a certified death certificate. Generally, the funeral home will immediately notify Social Security. However, you will need to follow up on this and make certain your questions are answered. You can go to the nearest Social Security Office or call the listed number. You also need to notify your mate's place of employment if he was working or receiving retirement benefits. If you were receiving a pension and/or any other benefits, such as insurance coverage, through your spouse's employer, contact the company as soon as possible to learn the status of your health insurance, hospitalization, and any other spousal benefits. These initial contacts cannot wait and should be accomplished within the week after your spouse died.

Life Insurance. You or your lawyer will also notify any life insurance companies holding policies on your spouse. Some businesses provide life insurance for an employee that takes effect at the time of death. This is in addition to insurance purchased by the individual. Claiming benefits on such policies usually requires a certified death certificate with the employee's name, company number, and Social Security number and might be handled through the employer. Any other life insurance policies, whether so-called "whole life" or "term life," also require a certified death certificate, as well as detailed information about the policy, including the policy number. You or your attorney or your insurance agent should find out what is needed to ensure prompt payment of benefits, and each insurance company will have to be contacted separately.

Do you know what county you reside in? You will have to familiarize yourself with numerous legal and official documents. Federal, state, county, or municipal laws guide some procedures. Determine where each of these transactions takes place, including probate of the will. It will make things much easier if you can have an attorney handle these legal and official documents.

Consider for Yourself

Ask Questions. You will interact with many government employees and professional people in the process of settling the estate. It is most important that you feel comfortable with any lawyer, accountant, broker, or physician, etc. with whom you are communicating. Do not hesitate to ask questions of them, and, if you do not understand the answers, ask again. Take notes whenever you talk to someone about an important issue. This is already a difficult time and some of these interviews or meetings may be quite trying, so this is not a good time to trust your memory of what is said. Just writing down the notes will help you determine whether you understand what is being said.

Consider and Reconsider. Most important, keep in mind that this is not a good time to make major decisions, financial or otherwise. While there is a lot that must be done, give yourself plenty of time to reconsider and get back to the big issues. In particular, most advisors and counselors advise that you not sell your house or move immediately. In fact, the standard advice is not to move for a year after you are widowed. You may regret a decision made too hastily. If it is necessary to move very soon after your loss, consider renting your house rather than selling.

While you are discussing and learning about your options, *do not give anyone complete control over your finances.* Get all the advice and help you need or can afford, but keep the ability to make final decisions for yourself. You can learn a lot and find answers by reading. The Internet or your local library or a good bookstore are useful sources of information. If nothing else, such reading may be dry enough to help you go to sleep at night.

Getting Down to Work

Getting Organized. Where will you work? Before you get down to work settling the estate, prepare a work area. Even if you are an accomplished computer maven, there will be a lot of documents to deal with and organize. Be certain that you have file folders, paper clips, note pads, postage stamps, pens, and pencils. Place pens conveniently in all areas where you are likely to use them—by each telephone, in your purse, your jacket pockets, on your night table. This will help as you acquire necessary information from many diverse sources as people return your calls or when you think of questions to ask later. Buy at least one roll of stamps so you won't have to return again and again to the post office. You will need many stamps for all your official correspondence, as well as for thank you notes.

Start your organization system by making a separate folder for each aspect of the estate you have to attend to. Always keep your work related to that issue in the appropriate folder, and include on the cover of the folder or inside the name of the company, the name of the person you speak with, the phone number and address, and appointment time. When filing your paper work, be certain to clarify what the company needs so you do not have to redo any applications or transfers.

Schedule Appointments. When you plan to meet with the banker, accountant, lawyer, or any of the various people who will try to assist you at this time, always schedule an appointment. It is a good strategy to be one of the first clients of the day, so that you will not have to wait.

Hardcopy Communications. Before sending information to companies, ask how they prefer mail or legal documents to be sent. Some of the various types of mail services you may use for legal documents in handling your estate papers are: express mail for overnight delivery service, certified mail for tracking a letter, restricted delivery to the addressee, or return receipt to assure you of delivery. While some communications may be handled by e-mail or FAX, anything requiring a direct signature requires a hardcopy. Further, using a hard copy permits you to make and keep a copy for your records and future reference. Generally, you will not send "express mail" to a P.O. Box, as it is delivered faster to a street address.

Special Mail. The U.S. Postal Service provides various forms you may need to mail documents by registered or certified or other special mail. If you have a few mailing forms on hand, you can fill them out before you leave home. Try to handle as much paper work from home as possible and avoid having to stand in line twice – once to get the forms and a second time to mail them. Be certain that your correct return address is on all the documents you mail; and also be certain that you have the correct zip code for everything you mail. Do not be in too big a hurry in preparing mailings. If you make hasty errors, it may actually slow down the process of completing your spouse's estate.

Thank You Notes. It is an excellent strategy to get a box of thank you note cards. The funeral home may provide some suitable cards, so try to remember to ask them about this. For each person who helps you with the estate, drop them a short note at once. They will remember this note from you and may even handle your paperwork with greater care, knowing that you appreciated their efforts. Everyone likes to be thanked and appreciated. An example of a brief note of thanks might read:

RE: Name and account number

Many thanks for processing the paper work on my spouse's insurance. Everyone today is overworked and I appreciate your taking the time to attend to this extra paper work at this difficult time of my life.

Sincerely,

This is just a rough draft, but it might help you with the wording.

Remember that the more organized you are and appear to others, the more receptive people will be to helping you or responding to your needs and requests. At this trying time, everyone should want to be helpful, but, in fact, you are one among many seeking his or her time. Show them you know how to handle yourself by having everything in order—and don't forget to write a thank you note.

Your Financial Affairs

Retain Your Options. Long term financial planning is not for the first few weeks of widowhood. However, you will need to establish your cash flow for immediate needs while you are trying to pull your life together. Unless someone else will handle all your financial affairs, you must look into your financial situation. Some widows may not know what their spouse's estate consists of in the way of bank accounts, stocks, property, etc. or there may be items that you have forgotten about. Whether you are confident of handling your financial affairs or not, do not forget the important concept noted above: *Do not give anyone complete control over your finances.* Get all the advice and help you feel you need or can afford, but retain the ability to make decisions for yourself.

Immediate Financial Tasks. There are some important and particularly immediate financial tasks. Basically you have to look at your immediate cash flow, the money to pay for the funeral, and your monthly expenses. The first things to examine are your checking and saving accounts, and possibly money market accounts, as these are the most liquid assets you can access. If you do not have enough money in these accounts, you may have to liquidate stocks, bonds, or other assets, so speak to your lawyer, accountant, or broker.

Checking Account. Is the checking account in your name so that you can continue to sign checks? If the account was only in your spouse's name, you need to know at once how to sign checks. How is this to be undertaken? Your lawyer will give you this information before probate and again after probate. Handling checks is critical to keep your cash flow intact. If your main bank account has an on-line "bill pay" feature, be certain that you can access and use it effectively.

Co-signer. On any bank account that has been jointly held, inquire as quickly as possible to make certain that your Social Security number is on it. Make an appointment with a banker and ask what the bank can do to help you. It is also important to get an alternate signature, perhaps an adult child or other close relative, authorized on your own checking and savings accounts. If you should become ill, someone will need to pay your bills and handle your financial business. If you transfer Social Security numbers on any account to your name, you can get signature cards for a new co-signer. This is a critical detail that you will not want to put off; handle this quickly.

Credit Cards. If there are credit cards that are only in your spouse's name, cancel them immediately. Some companies may transfer such accounts over to you but generally will not accept a charge from you on your spouse's card. Making these changes will probably require a copy of the death certificate. Check to see if your spouse had insurance that paid off the credit card balance in case of his death.

Value of the estate

You need to determine the value of the estate on the day your spouse died. This means the value of each stock and bond and the appraised value of property. Your lawyer needs to determine the value of the estate, and the more of this information you can provide, the less the legal fee will be for his or her services. Ascertaining values on the exact date of death may involve looking at numerous items and gathering quite a bit of information. Be certain that you make a folder on the value of the estate at the date of death (or closest business day).

As you get the pieces that make up the whole, list them, keeping all of these valuation documents in one folder. Alternately, you may prefer to start a file in your computer that lists assets and their values.

To start the process, especially if you are not aware of all of your holdings, refer to the previous year's income tax form. Since all your sources of taxable income should be on this tax statement, it has a complete list of all income reported, and it names the various banks, stockbrokers, and income property. This provides a good beginning to help you at the present time. In preparing the value of your estate, start with a list of all of your bank accounts and related accounts. Call the banks and give them the date of your spouse's death and ask for the balance on that date. Your list might look something like this example:

<u>Balance on date of death</u>

First State Bank Acct # .... $ ____.__

First National Bank Acct # .... ____.__

If you have a stockbroker, then call and make an appointment to see him or her soon, if the office is local. If you deal with out-of-town brokers, handle this on the phone. Ask the brokers to prepare, on company letterhead, an itemized list with the value of the entire account on the date of death. This will serve as a document for the probate court process. An example might look like this:

<u>Balance on date of death</u>

Stock of .... $ ____.__

Bonds of .... ____.__

Other accounts ____.__

Total value of stocks or other assets at date of death $ ____.__

Appraisals. Do you have written appraisals on your spouse's jewelry, art, or personal effects? If so, such appraisals can be used to help place a value on this portion of the assets. If you do not have previous appraisals, have your property insurance company outline these items in a letter, which might be acceptable. To determine the value of your spouse's car, check the so-called "blue book" on the Internet or at the public library or ask your auto dealer to help with the valuation. If you received an income tax refund in the year your spouse passes away, that is also part of the estate.

Talk to your CPA about having your home appraised. Your lawyer will need this information for probate, and your heirs will need this house valuation if they later sell the home upon your death. Also, if you sell your residence to move elsewhere, your profit is based on the new value at the time of spouse's death, not on the original purchase price. A real estate agent may help determine the current value, for a nominal charge, or an actual appraiser can handle this professionally. Your accountant can advise you with this

If there are U.S. Savings Bonds in your spouse's name, your bank can assist you setting the actual value at time of death. If the bonds have matured or are close to maturity, your state may allow face value to be used. If any U.S. Savings Bonds were only in your spouse's name, you will need to wait until you have received a letter (also known as a Letter of Testamentary) stating that you are the executor or executrix of the will. Take this letter, along with a certified copy of the death certificate, to the bank. A bank employee will help you transfer these bonds into your name. You will have to leave copies of both papers with the bank, so be certain you have plenty of extra copies of everything.

Automobiles. If your spouse's car or your family car was in his/her name only, you will need to transfer the car title to your name. To accomplish this, once again take a certified death certificate and the letter naming you as the executrix of the estate to the county clerk's office. They will handle the paper work. Be sure you take cash, check or a credit card with you, as there is a fee for this title transfer.

As you plan to make these trips to the bank or courthouse, etc., remember to call ahead and make certain you are going to the correct location. If your city has a substation courthouse, this will be easiest to use, unless you are planning a trip downtown. Try to go early on a Tuesday morning, as they are not usually as busy on that day.

Retirement Funds. If your spouse had an Individual Retirement Account (IRA) or any tax-sheltered annuity or other self-directed retirement fund, it is essential to have these funds put into a rollover account. If this is taken as a lump-sum payout, you are likely to incur sizeable tax penalties, so be certain to look into this carefully or instruct your accountant or financial planner to take care of it. Also, be certain to learn whether the rollover monies will start a new time-line in the new account based on your age or birth date.

Lawyers and Legal Concerns

Among your priorities is to schedule a meeting with your lawyer as soon as possible after your husband's funeral. For the first meeting after you are widowed, try to take an adult child or other close family member along with you, as this is a trying experience for all. If possible, have the lawyer who wrote your spouse's will handle the estate. It may be best for the heirs to know that you used your spouse's lawyer, even if he or she is not your personal attorney.

Executor or Executrix. If you are named the executor or executrix of your spouse's will, this means you are to carry out all provisions of the will and to disperse the assets as outlined. If you are not the sole heir at this time, you and your lawyer can work out the arrangements. Each state has various laws and only a lawyer can apprise you of distribution methods. If possible, give each of your adult children a copy of your spouse's will, so they are immediately aware of how the estate is to be handled. It is a particularly good idea to distribute copies of the will if there are children from more than one family involved.

Probate. When meeting with the lawyer to probate the will, ask the fee up front. Some states do not allow attorneys to charge a percentage of the estate, and the lawyer will give you an hourly rate. Ask how many hours this is expected to require and approximately what the total cost will be. If state law allows the attorney to charge a percentage of the estate, then accept only the method that is less, the hourly rate or the percentage. This should be your choice.

Power of Attorney. Does someone have power of attorney for you, in case you should become disabled? This is another priority for you, as a widow, to arrange. What if an illness strikes you? Who will pay your bills, handle legal matters, or make your investments? Discuss this with your lawyer quickly. The lawyer may put this on the back burner, but don't let it be delayed. We never want to think of our own sicknesses, especially when we have just lost our spouse. Life has to be lived on a real and daily basis. Anyone can become disabled from a fall, accident, or stroke. Get your power of attorney appointed, and explain to your family who it is and why you chose him or her, so there is no problem and no confusion if such a catastrophe should occur.

Your Own Will. You may need to rewrite your own will as quickly as possible. In most cases, your spouse was to be the beneficiary of your own estate. With the death of your spouse, your will may be invalid, and upon your death your estate may not be handled as you wish.

Before you visit your attorney, write out what you want in the way of the disposal of your home, car, and personal effects. Most lawyers charge by the hour, and the more preparation you do, the less you will be charged. Anything that takes up the lawyer's time should be written down before your session. Give the attorney a written list of your heirs, their addresses and phone numbers, as well as a list of your properties.

Decisions about disposal of the major financial part of your estate are the most important at the moment. Discuss living trusts or other trusts with your lawyer. Depending on the size of your estate, consult your lawyer and CPA to assure that the bulk of your estate goes to your heirs and not to the government. If you want to leave special items, such as heirlooms, jewelry, silver, or works of art to specific family members and friends, this can be added in a letter when you have more time in the future.

Probate Court

Generally, wills have to be filed in probate court, depending on state and local laws. Probate is a specialized court or division of a state trial court that considers only cases concerning the distribution of a person's estate. This court generally examines the authenticity of a will and determines who receives property under state law. A probate judge oversees procedures to pay a deceased person's debts and to distribute the assets to the proper inheritors.

In some states, if you have a trust fund, you may be able to bypass probate court. But if you are the sole executrix of your spouse's estate, you and your lawyer will probably make a date to register or present the will in your county probate court.

Your court date may be a challenging day; so if you feel that you need support, ask a family member or close friend to go with you. If you go by yourself and are not familiar with the court house location, call ahead to find out where to park the car so that you do not waste time looking for a parking spot. Also, carry plenty of change, because if you park at a meter or a parking lot, you are likely to need small coins.

Your attorney should have all appropriate papers prepared and the appointment time set up. First, he or she will admit the will to probate with a document and a certified death certificate. Assuming that you are the executrix, you will be administered an oath which states that you will perform the duties as the independent executrix of the estate. There is little for you to do or say, as the attorney and judge do most of the talking. However, as you place the will in probate, this experience is likely to reinforce the fact you have been widowed,

Several documents will be given to the county clerk for filing. Your lawyer will publish in a local commercial newspaper the fact that this will is in probate so that creditors are legally advised. The judge will grant you a "letter of testamentary," which will allow you to transfer all assets (such as savings bonds, stock, bank accounts, house, car, etc.) and debts into your name. Any assets that did not have you listed as the owner or co-owner of said property can be titled to you as an individual with the letter of testamentary.

The details of the documents and arrangements you can expect to encounter may vary by county or state, but the above is brief idea of your day in probate court.

Tax Matters

Income Taxes. If you have employed a CPA, call and ask advice on anything immediate. If he or she can give you a rough estimate of what your taxes will be, it is best to get this information as soon as possible. For the first year after or during which your spouse died, you can still file federal income taxes as a couple, which will help your tax status. You will want to be certain to have adequate funds allocated to pay your federal and state taxes, as well as any property taxes, when they come due, as you do not want to waste money on penalties for late payment.

Property Taxes. In some cities, if you are over 65 you are entitled to a property tax exemption for senior citizens. If your home has been listed only in your spouse's name, have this changed to your name. Check with the county and city tax appraiser's office as to how this is handled. They may need a copy of your driver's license to prove your age and a copy of the death certificate to finalize the change to your name.

Social Security

Notify the Social Security Administration as quickly as possible after your spouse's death, as noted above. This might be handled by telephone, or possibly over the Internet, but it is preferable to go to the nearest Social Security office in person so that you can more readily get all your questions answered. It is also a good idea to ask for copies of any paperwork generated. The agency staff will make copies for you, but often only if you ask.

For your spouse's record, the Social Security Administration will need the date of death, date of birth, and his/her Social Security number, and your Social Security number. If you are already drawing Social Security on your own record, you may become eligible to receive more. If your spouse's benefit was higher than yours, you should be entitled to receive the difference.

Dealing with the Social Security Administration, or any other big bureaucratic organization, can be a stressful experience, even when you are not grieving. Do realize that many people dealing with this agency feel such stress. However, you do have to deal with the red tape of Social Security and other institutions. The best approach to make things as smooth as possible is to have a good file or notebook with all the relevant information to take with you on your visits. Call the office before you go and determine exactly what you need to take and what documents they will need. Then, when you are there, be certain to write down the names of everyone you talk to or who helps you and also their direct phone numbers or extension numbers, so that you can follow up with additional questions.

Keeping your files in order will really pay off in your interactions with government agencies. Remember that the government employees you talk with see so many clients every day that they cannot be expected to remember you. You have to keep track of your own interests. And that thank you note will help too.

Insurance

House and Car Insurance. Notify your home owners-insurance and automobile-insurance companies of your spouse's death. These insurance policies have to be changed to your name only. Also, ask if there is any pro rated rebate due to you on pre-paid premiums (it never hurts to ask if money is owed you). You will want to remove your spouse's jewelry and personal effects from any household insurance policies as soon as you dispose of these items. Be sure to get a premium rebate when removing items from this policy.

Life Insurance. You or your lawyer will need to notify the life insurance companies where your spouse had policies related to his death. If you are handling this sometimes-complex process, each company will tell you how they handle this, as they are all different. Keep each company file in a separate folder marked with the company name, phone number, address, and the individual you talked with. You will probably need a certified death certificate for each one. Generally life insurance companies will accept only a *certified* copy of a death certificate. Remember, there is a difference between a certified death certificate and a copy.

Health Insurance. If you had any private health insurance policies, ask for a refund on premiums already paid for your spouse. Do not close out this folder until the refund is all settled; claim any insurance refund due to you. Also, some credit cards or bank accounts have a life insurance policy offered as a freebie to get your business. Find out whether any financial assets or accounts may have carried such a policy. This may bring unexpected insurance monies to you, but you will have to follow up and file for it in each case.

Medicare and Medical Insurance Claims

You will now assume the responsibility for all Medicare or other medical insurance payments and insurance claims. For full explanations of Medicare benefits, you can go on-line or contact the Medicare section of the Social Security Administration.

If you have Medicare coverage, your doctor, by law, must file with Medicare. However, you may first have to pay the outstanding bill, and then Medicare will reimburse you. It is a good idea to check the payment procedure with each doctor before you go for an appointment, so you understand which procedure he or she uses. Generally, doctors will also file with any secondary insurance you have. If you file directly with secondary insurance, you wait until Medicare sends you the notice of how much they paid the physician and then follow up with the physician or hospital office to make certain all claims are covered.

It may be best to keep two medical claims files: one of open claims and one of closed claims. Keep these files on an annual basis with a new file each year. Review open claims periodically, regardless of what people say. Medicare is reasonably timely about paying the bills from doctors. To avoid a hold-up from the doctor's office, you may have to keep a close watch on all the paper work. If you use an HMO or you do not yet have Medicare coverage, it will be most helpful if you learn the exact procedures from your HMO or insurance office.

If you learn how each doctor or hospital or other healthcare provider utilizes Medicare, HMOs, and insurance, you will be able to minimize any medical-claims problems and also minimize the amounts you have to pay out-of-pocket. It is of utmost importance that you keep track of your medical bills correctly, as it is not unusual for problems or issues to arise.

Changed Travel Plans

Perhaps you had a trip in the works. This needs to be cancelled as soon as possible with the airlines, the hotel, or travel agent. They will need a copy of the death certificate along with the tickets. Keep a copy of everything. Also, send items like this registered mail with a return receipt requested, so you will know that these valuable items were received. Each airline has different rules, so call and inquire about the best procedure.

If your spouse had any airline miles accumulated, the airline should transfer them and credit your account with his accumulated mileage. This is one of the few things that should be easy to handle. Although each airline is different, most will accept a copy of the death certificate along with the account number. Keep this separate folder open until you actually receive the next statement showing the transfer transaction is complete.

You should be able to call any airline on a local or toll-free 800-phone number. There is an 800 information system you can call to get numbers [1-800-555-1212]. When you call an airline, be certain that you are talking to the right department or person; you don't want to have to go into great detail more than once to get the necessary changes made. For other previously made plans (vacation or business) be certain to cancel all reservations and to ask explicitly for a refund if there was any deposit or down payment. And, as always, be certain to write out exactly what you have to send in for each type of transaction.

SECTION FOUR
IT'S YOUR HOME

Some things ... arrive in their own mysterious hour, on their own terms
and not yours, to be seized or relinquished forever.

Gail Godwin,
The Quotable Woman, page 146

Remaining in Your Home

Many experts agree that someone newly widowed will be able
to regain her or his equilibrium best by remaining in the same familiar
surroundings for at least a year, if this is possible. Staying in place
allows you to retain the sense of familiarity with your surroundings
that has provided support in the past. This is a good time to stay put
until you have a positive reason to seek a change when you are ready
to enter the next phase of your own life.

Remaining in your current home also allows you to maintain
the support systems in your community with which you are familiar
and comfortable. In particular, your physician, dentist, pharmacy, and
minister, priest or rabbi, and other professionals will be accessible on
the same basis. It will also be easier to venture out to your familiar
grocery, laundry, and the other locations that have been part of your
usual routines.

Even though you remain in the same place, it will not be the
same environment. If you did not live with other family members
besides your spouse, the entire space is now yours to consider, to
occupy, and to rearrange. Now, it is the time to take a good look
around the space you live in, whether it is a large home or a small
apartment. Keep your eyes wide open as you look at and think about
each room and the space within each room and how it can best serve
your own needs. However, there are some things to do that cannot be
postponed, and home is the place to start.

Disposing of Things

Stop and consider whether it will be easier for you to face the
necessary tasks of sorting your spouse's things by yourself or with a

family member or friend there to lend support. This is a very personal question, and you will find your own answer to do what is most comfortable for you. But this is also a task that your children, no matter what age they are, may also feel very sensitive about. They may find that helping you with this process allows them to move through the grieving process, as well as feeling that they are able to support you.

As you are going through your spouse's personal effects, sort out certain things you think children, grandchildren, friends, or others would like. For example, chess sets, golf clubs or tennis racquets, coin or stamp collections, miniature cars, or whatever you feel reflects your spouse can be given to that certain person with a card telling the recipient that it is "from Grandpa's Treasures" or however the recipient was associated. This is a nice remembrance for those receiving the memento.

If there is a very young child or grandchild, think about saving something special, like a watch or piece of jewelry, for when the child gets older. You might want to have the item cleaned and checked by a jeweler to prepare it for storage for several years.

Medical Items and Medicines

Medic Alert System. Was your spouse on a medic alert system? If he/she was a diabetic, had a pace maker, or any illness for which he belonged to medic alert, call the company and get this canceled at once. If he wore medic alert jewelry, you may be able to return this item to be used for someone unable to purchase one.

Medications. Dispose of any of your spouse's remaining medicines as soon as possible. If he was a diabetic, you may be able to donate any remaining unopened supplies and certainly any reference books to the diabetic center at a hospital or clinic. These may be used by other people and will be dispersed properly. Call your local pharmacy about any unopened and sealed medications. They can advise you if this can be used by any health center. Carefully dispose of all open medicines; take the labels from the bottles and dispose of the labels separately from the bottles so no one else can get the numbers. Remember to notify the pharmacy that your spouse is deceased and not to issue these prescriptions to anyone.

Items to Donate

Automobile. If your spouse had a car that you will no longer need or use, you will want to dispose of it as soon as you can get to it. You can sell it directly to an individual, but this may involve allowing strangers to test drive the car, which is not always a safe procedure. Alternately, you can sell it to a used car dealer and reduce your potential hazard. Or, you can donate it to a national organization that will give you a receipt for a tax deduction and will then sell it for fund raising. The national Kidney Foundation is one such option, and they will come tow away the car at no charge to you.

Clothing. You may find new clothing in checking your spouse's wardrobe. If so, return these items to the store where they were purchased and request a refund or store credit for them. You can receive tax deductions for giving lightly worn clothing and household goods to your favorite charity. Goodwill Industries, the Veterans Administration, the Salvation Army, many church clothing closets, and other non-profit organizations will recycle gently worn clothing to those in need.

Magazines. If your spouse subscribed to magazines related to his hobby or special activities and you do not want these any longer, call or write or e-mail the circulation departments of the magazines. Be certain to include an address label with your letter or the information from the label in your e-mail, as this will give them additional subscription reference numbers. Ask them to stop the magazine and refund any monies due on the subscription. This means another file to keep in a separate folder until you receive the letter and the cancellation rebate.

Special Items or Books. If your spouse had a hobby and had a library collection associated with it, you may want to dispose of these books. It may be that a child, grandchild, or other relative or friend would love to have these mementos; but if the family's interests are different, you can call the public library and donate these books. If there are a lot of heavy books, they may have a volunteer pick them up from your home. They will give you a receipt for an income tax deduction, and just think of how many people will be made happy by reading and referring to the books your spouse used in his hobby.

Eyeglasses. If you have eyeglasses of your spouse's, don't throw them away. You can put them to good use by donating them to the local Lion's Club chapter. They recycle eyeglasses for individuals who cannot afford them. Many optical shops have boxes where you can deposit these glasses, or check in the yellow pages for the eye glasses depository and drop them off.

Getting Started

You may want to change the telephone directory listing to your name. You might consider using only your initials, so that it is not apparent that a single woman has this phone number. You may also need to change the message on your answering machine, if you use one. Or now may be the time to start using an answering machine so that you can screen calls and overlook those you do not wish to answer. On a positive note, you might begin your new message with a cheerful greeting, such as "Aloha" or "Shalom." Think up a greeting that represents you.

Have your spouse's name removed from any mailing lists or databases that generate mail that does not interest you. Sadly, you can often do this by writing "deceased, return to sender" on the envelope and putting it back in a mail box; you can even return bulk mail items this way. The post office will also give you a form to complete to get off many mail lists.

Be aware that this difficult time for you is just the time that unscrupulous individuals and businesses select to prey on those who are grieving. Do not sign any orders for anything, such as home repairs, at this time, or pay for anything that arrives COD unless you were already aware of the order and still want the merchandise.

Around the House

Do you know how to use all the electronic and other equipment in your home? If there is equipment you have not yet mastered, now is the time to get out the instruction manual or to get someone to teach you. Just make up your mind to get the hang of each gadget and make it useful, or get rid of it.

It is a very good safety and security idea to keep several flashlights in various rooms. The lights do go out on occasion. When you are alone, it is good to know you have flashlights handy during storms or anytime the electricity goes out. Either check the batteries on a regular basis to be sure they are working or you can get flashlights that are recharged by plugging them in for a period of time.

In addition, you now are in charge of everything that uses a battery. Unless you are mechanically inclined, which many of you are, this may be a bigger job than you think. Get someone to show you how to change the batteries on the following: flashlights, clocks, garage door opener, cameras, and battery-operated games. There is nothing worse than needing to use one of these items and finding that you can't quite figure it out. "Be prepared" is always a good motto.

Electrical fuses in the house may be even more important than batteries. Be certain that you know where the fuse box is, especially in an older home, and how to use it. In addition, you may now be responsible for changing all of the light bulbs on your property. This includes all sorts of things besides just the easy lamps; there are yard lights, front and back porch lights, fixtures with covers, and other kinds of lights you probably didn't realize you have. You may need a good sturdy ladder for the hard-to-reach bulbs or get someone to help you handle this task.

For starters, why don't you check around the house for the various sizes of batteries, fuses, and light bulbs you use and make a list of them? Then you can make one trip to the store to get a reasonable supply of all sizes. Now you will be ready for those inconvenient times when something invariably goes out at the worst possible time.

SECTION FIVE

YOUR OWN NEW LIFE

Birds sing after a storm; why shouldn't people feel as free
to delight in whatever remains to them?

Rose Kennedy,
The Quotable Woman, page 148

Think of the positive side of being on your own. There are some positives. In your new life, you may cater to your own whims and "just do it your way." Also, make an effort to think positive thoughts at least some of the time; or set aside a special time each day to meditate on the most serene and positive things you can imagine.

Life is a mixture of positives and negatives, good and bad. In your present circumstances, the negative part is the loss of your spouse, but you can also find positive aspects of your new life. The following statement will perhaps make you either sad or mad, but it is true ... *you can now do things to suit yourself.* This may be a difficult thought, but it is true, and trying to shape a positive outlook will help.

Think of some of the ways you can now suit yourself around the house:

1. You can set the temperature in the house and car to please your body.

2. The window blinds can be opened or closed; you please yourself on this.

3. Fans can be turned on or off in the evening when you sleep. No more worrying if the air is "ruffling" your mate while you are stifled or visa-versa.

4. You can go to the movie of your choice or watch the TV show that you prefer. No more worrying about watching a "chick flick" when this might have been annoying to your husband.

5. Perhaps you cooked basically to please your mate. Now you can cook exactly what you like or what's best for your diet.

For Yourself

Daily activities may be nicer if you have sheets and towels that you have not shared with your spouse. So, you may wish to get some new sheets and towels as soon as possible. You are in a new stage of your life and this change can help. If you prefer to cling to things you shared, this idea may not be for you, but give it a thought.

Music can add much to your life now. Did you ever play an instrument or sing in a choir? If you have been neglecting these things, now is a good time to put music back into your life. Maybe you can work in a school as a volunteer and help in the music department, or what about entertaining at a nursing home with your guitar or violin?

Perhaps you have always wanted to study art and had no time. Now you may have time. Join an art appreciation class at a local museum or college. Many of these are on Sunday, which is likely to be a lonely day if you do not have family nearby. You can spend hours learning and enjoying the masters of art.

Go out to eat. Try eating breakfast out, if you don't usually like to go to lunch or dinner alone. Take the newspaper or a book and read it. When you go to a restaurant alone, expect to be treated with the same courtesy and to receive the same good service as you do when you are with someone else or with a group. Your business should be important to the restaurant, even if you are a single diner. Also, don't neglect to tip a reasonable amount for the service you receive.

Enjoy some special pleasure each day, just for yourself. This may be something as little as a bubble bath or trying a new hand lotion. This may entail sampling a new flavor of coffee and a cookie when you take a break, but it will help you recognize that you are special.

You might choose to select new sleeping garments,

nightgowns or pajamas, whatever you prefer. Try a new style or develop a different outfit with something already in your closet; find the new you.

Do try to cut or buy yourself fresh flowers once a week, even if it is only a sprig from the yard or one rose or two carnations. A flower adds something bright, cheerful, and alive to your house. Or get balloons and put them in different rooms. Don't be afraid to bring joy and brightness into your home.

Invite friends over, or consider hosting a small get-together, a Sunday brunch, cocktails, or an informal party. Your married friends may feel awkward, unsure how to talk about your loss. If you lead the way, they are more likely to include you in their future plans for an evening out. At first, your married friends who care about you, will perhaps invite you for dinner and include you when they plan an outing. Soon, however, they are likely to resume their lives in their "couples' world." That's okay. You don't want to feel like a third wheel.

It is incumbent upon you to seek new acquaintances, people with a variety of interests. Get to know men, women, and children who are younger and older than you, people who express different ideas about the world. When you go to church, travel, or attend a book club, start conversations with people older and younger than yourself. They will enrich your life during this time of potential loneliness. The biggest mistake bereaved people make is to stay within their own comfort zone. Break out of the circle. Age should not define your friends.

Make your home and living environment come to life. Decorate your house for all of the holidays or at least put something on your table for each holiday. Try a Valentine centerpiece; put a shamrock on the front door; fly a flag for the Fourth of July, even if it is a small one. It feels festive to set the table with holiday napkins. Use your own judgment, but try to celebrate as many holidays as feasible in your home. This helps to mark time, to keep track of the seasons, and to add variety to potentially lonely days. Remember that you are important and you deserve to celebrate each day of your life.

You may find a friend who likes to do different things than you care about, and it may work to "swap chores" with him or her. Perhaps she likes to plant flowers or trim shrubs, and you prefer to do insurance claims. Maybe you like to bake and she likes to run errands in the car. Trade out with one another to do the things you think are fun (or the least onerous), and then your friend can do what she thinks is enjoyable. This will help build friendships and give you an opportunity to use your abilities to their fullest.

As difficult as it may seem, the best thing you can plan to do is take a trip as soon as possible. This could be to visit your grown children or a friend in another city, but you need to get away from home for a few days, to sleep in another bed, and to experience other surroundings. This may sound difficult at this time, but it will be worth the effort. However, when making plans, you will probably want to start with a relatively short trip or tour.

After that initial trip, you will doubtless be glad to return to your own space, and life will seem a little brighter and possibly easier. It may still be lonely, but your body and brain will have had time to relax. That is important to your recovery process. And later on, don't be afraid to try traveling to some place you would really like to visit ... you can still have fun as a widow. You have a life to live, and travel can be a part of that life.

Exercise

Don't stop exercising. If you have not been in the habit of exercising, start as soon as possible. Joining a health club may be the best idea, as it gets you up, dressed, and out with people. Staying at home and using an exercise CD or jogging on equipment in your home may not be the best for now, because you need to be out and about. This gets both your body and mind working.

Taking a walk each day is such an easy thing to work into your routine. It feels good and gives you a great feeling of accomplishment and has no cost. It will help you to feel good if you accomplish something healthful early in the day to get you started. What a great new adventure to start...walking and letting your brain wander to figure out how to live this new life. While you are walking outdoors is also a good time to look around at things you might not have paid much attention to before - grass, leaves, automobiles you pass, or shop windows, street signs, etc.

Do you know how to swim? This is wonderful exercise that you can do at a local "Y" or a health club. The water is soothing, uses all of your muscles and gets the blood circulating. If you don't know how to swim, now is a good time to learn, so sign up for lessons. If you are already an accomplished swimmer, you might volunteer to teach young people who are disabled or cannot afford standard lessons how to swim.

Yoga provides another great possibility at any age and stage. Find a class or group and sign up. Yoga leaves you refreshed, with your mind clear and ready for decision making. You do not have to commit to a long series of classes. Start with one hour a week. Another possibility for combining entertainment or socializing with exercise is to find a dance class or dancing group. Ballroom dancing is "in" and often there are classes available for singles at the "Y" or through a social organization. Also, line dancing is good exercise and can be done with any size or group mix, rather than partners.

Pets

Having a pet provides companionship. If you are not a dog or cat lover and do not want the responsibility of tending to an animal, think about having a fish or a bird as a pet. Colorful fish will add much to your home. A bird chirping will make your house feel alive. Many pets can be trained and that will give you a feeling of accomplishment. Other small animals, such as a gerbil, a rabbit or even a turtle, can become rewarding pets. Or, for the more adventurous, consider horseback riding.

If you have any outdoor space, install a birdhouse, a bird feeder, or even a birdbath. You will truly enjoy the wildlife coming into your yard each day. Helping wild animals nurture their families will bring living and joy into your life with little effort on your part.

If you already have and enjoy a pet, then you understand this daily lift. If you have a dog, now is an opportune time to join a dog-obedience class or take a refresher or advanced course. A trained pet helps you enjoy life more, and you will feel closer to it, because you are working partners.

If you are good with animals, you and your pet may even train for volunteer work. Several national organizations sponsor training programs for dogs and cats to help the blind, the elderly, and emotionally disturbed youngsters. You might explore taking on the responsibility of training your pet to help someone with special needs. Alternately, you can adopt a "rescued" animal from a local animal shelter or organization.

On the other hand, realize that pets require continuing care and costs. Do not let anyone give you a pet unless you are quite certain that you are able to care for it on a daily basis.

Security

Make your home and car and environment safe and secure havens. Do call the police in your area, but not on 911 unless it is real emergency. The police have an office for non-emergencies. Advise them that you are newly widowed and alone. Get their advice on leaving lights on outside and learn about any protection they might offer. If you have a neighborhood patrol, ask them to check on your house more often than usual if possible. You will feel more secure.

This is a good time to install a telephone answering machine, if you do not already have one. The message you have on it should be brief and clear, perhaps "this is 123-4567, please leave a message at the tone." You can also use the answering machine to screen your calls, even when you are at home. Do not say anything in your message to indicate that you live alone. In fact, women may want to have a male relative or friend recite the message on the answering machine so that strangers and sales people who phone will have no indication that you are a single woman living alone.

If you do not have a cordless telephone or a cell phone, now is the time to acquire one. For your security and peace of mind, this is a must when you live alone as there is no one else to answer the phone for you. No matter what room you are in, or what you are doing, have a phone with you. Remember to put the phone by your bed at night and to slip it in your pocket if you are out in the yard or even using the apartment elevator.

Call a locksmith to come and check all of your locks, patio doors, and your garage. Locksmiths often make good suggestions about home safety. If you don't have a lock on your bedroom door, you may want to have one installed for extra protection. If someone should break in, this bedroom door lock gives you extra time to reach your security system, if you have one, or to call 911. However, just in case you get sick, be sure to give an extra bedroom key to a neighbor or family member. And always be sure that you can exit the house easily in case of emergency.

Your Car

Take your cell phone in the car, especially whenever you travel alone. It is truly a necessity, not a luxury. If you are late or early to a meeting or appointment, you can notify the doctor, the dentist, or whomever you are going to visit. If you have car trouble, wherever you might be, you cannot leave your car and you do not want to be stranded. Most cell phones have a number you can dial to get emergency or special assistance. Also, consider joining an automobile club, like the American Automobile Association (AAA), to provide an extra measure of security. For an annual fee, AAA responds to emergency calls for assistance from your home or from the roadside.

Don't run out of gas. You have no one to remind you to check the fuel gauge and no one to help you if you run out of gas on the road. If you note when your tank is half full, that can be your signal to fill up soon. Your mind is on so many other things to do that you may easily postpone filling up the tank. Don't delay this task. It is an important safety precaution and convenience to keep your car fueled correctly.

Get regular diagnostic check ups for your car. Then you will not have surprises or car trouble that may be lurking just when you are busiest. If your car is under warranty, go to the dealer's service manager and ask for explanations about any previous maintenance and repair work done on your car. Explain that you are now alone and want to familiarize yourself with car maintenance schedules. It is up to you to become aware so that you are not taken advantage of with extra repairs. Caring for your car may seem a big responsibility or a nuisance, but you can avoid problems by thinking and planning ahead. Assert yourself before your car's next check up.

Eating

When it comes to eating, it is best not to be a "grazer" for very long. Many widows and widowers eat incorrectly at first, because they may no longer have regularly scheduled meal times. There is so much food that people bring to the house. We all eat wrong at first. Do not let this become a habit. It may be too much trouble to prepare appropriate healthful foods. Perhaps this is one of the hardest tasks for you to tackle, but your diet is very important. It affects how you feel each day and impacts your health over time.

Each individual's diet is different. Ask your doctor or a nutritionist what you need to eat to maintain your health and normal weight. Discuss how many calories, much fat, how much calcium, etc., you need a day and stick to this. Prepare your dinner early in the day. Fix your salad, bread, a chicken breast or fish filet and have it ready to pop in the oven or microwave later that evening when you are ready for dinner. This will get you off to a good start of balanced meals.

Each day, try to plan mentally or list what you will eat the next day and write it down. Stick to this approach. Then, you will know what you have planned to eat without too much thinking at the actual time. Don't eat standing up, as that is not a meal. To enhance your desire to actually sit down at the table, select a placemat and cloth napkin; use a pretty place setting of china. Pour a glass of wine if you desire, light a candle, watch your favorite TV show or read a book, and learn to enjoy eating alone. Sometimes, eat dinner in a different area - on the patio, in the den, in front of the fireplace. .

As Ralph Edwards, a television host from the 1950s, used to say, "This is your life." It may not be the life you chose at this time, but eating correctly will give you a chance to lead a healthy life, and this is what you want. Eating correctly is difficult and yet so important to help you move forward into your new circumstances.

Your Health

Make a List. If you take medicine on a daily basis, make a careful list of your doctors, medications, and prescription numbers as well as dosages. Tape the list to the inside of your medicine cabinet.

This will greatly assist anyone helping you if you should become ill or enter a hospital. Think ahead and take charge of your own health.

Don't get hooked on sleeping pills. If sleeping becomes a major problem, ask your doctor about the over-the-counter medicines that designate P.M. Most of these contain Benadryl as a soothing agent and are not habit forming.

Don't start drinking cups and cups of coffee, or cans and cans of soft drinks. These will rob you of sleep and nutrition. You must keep your system in good shape, so drink the "old faithful" - water. Keep a glass or small bottle of water handy and sip on this all daylong and even at night if you are awake. Water will help your nervousness and also your health. Remember, protect your health at this time; nothing is of more critical importance.

Watch for hormonal changes while you are in a period of grief. Many things can be affected by your emotional state: your teeth, a yeast infection, a bladder infection. Your body is undergoing a big shock. Don't be afraid to see your doctor if you don't feel well. He or she will be understanding and make suggestions for you.

Be careful not to run out of your favorite lotions, muscle relaxants, feminine hygiene products, or over-the- counter pain relievers that you use. You don't want to call for help from friends and family over a personal item that you can keep on hand. Only call your friends for real emergencies.

Sometimes, despite your vigilance, you will inevitably get sick. Let's hope your illnesses are minor, but be prepared at home. Keep on hand certain foods you might need to treat a sore throat or a stomach ache. These might include a clear-color carbonated drink, chicken soup, an electrolyte drink, pudding mix, gelatin mix, plain instant oatmeal, powdered milk, and canned juice. All of these are good to have on hand when you catch cold or suffer from a 24-hour stomach virus.

While none of us want to think about contracting a major illness, this can happen at any time. Isn't it best to have a contingency plan to fall back on? Research a responsible nursing agency, then call to learn what type of help is available if you ever need it. If you are on Medicare, know the benefits offered in the way of home nursing care and home help. You will be relieved if you know your rights and what is available before you need to use special help. You might also try to figure out where a nurse or friend could stay in your home if you needed help for a night or two or even longer. Not everyone has a spare bedroom, so develop a tentative plan.

Get Organized

If you should become ill, someone unfamiliar with your household will have to help you. Keep an updated list all of your doctors in your address book under "doctors." Clearly list each physician's name, specialty, address, and phone number. Under "household," list everyone you call to help run your home, such as a maid, plumber, heating and air conditioning companies, yard help, tree trimmer, etc. For insurance companies, be sure to list your account number, your agent, and their address and phone number. Then, remember to go over this list with the relative or person who would be in charge of paying your bills if you became ill.

While you are at it, go ahead and make a copy of this list for each of your adult children or any other close relative who might handle your affairs if necessary. Include contact information about your attorney, stockbroker, CPA, and any other professionals your use. Either list your major assets, checking and savings bank names and account numbers, and the attorney who should take care of your will, or tell your children where this information can readily be found.

Enjoy Your Activities

If you like to bake, but cannot eat all of that rich food, deliver the extra cookies or brownies to your local post office or nearby fire department. It will be such a surprise to these special people, as they are seldom remembered in such a personal manner. Look for a great big smile the next time you are at the post office. Delivering sweet treats can fill up a good portion of an otherwise dreary day and lift your spirits high.

Lucky for you if you can knit or sew. Start a project that requires a few stitches each day, or join a group, like a quilters' association, that works on special projects for others. As the days go by, you will see your progress on some shawl or quilt, and this will make you feel fulfilled. The project will become something to look forward to each day. Do something easy, as now is not the time to try something too complicated. Relax and enjoy.

Try to answer your phone with a cheery tone. This will make you happy, or at the very least it will make you feel better. Say "Happy Saturday," "Happy Ground Hog Day" if it is February 2, "Happy Super Bowl Day" if it is the day of the big game. What about "Happy Chinese New Year?" Think of something fun to say to keep your spirits up and to keep yourself abreast of the changing seasons.

Volunteer to tutor at your neighborhood elementary school. Schools often look for adults to read, one-on-one, with students who have fallen behind. Get a pen pal program going with a student at a local or even a far away school. Most elementary schools will welcome this suggestion and be glad to select a student who may benefit from a relationship with an interested adult. Perhaps you can arrange to have lunch with these students in the school cafeteria. Fill some time during your days by reaching out to someone younger than you who needs a friend. You can be that friend.

You don't feel like reading aloud or writing letters? What about e-mailing your family and friends? Grandchildren love to get cheery, personal e-mails. You can re-establish friendships with people you haven't seen in ages by sending an e-mail. It doesn't take long to stay in touch this way. Reach out with a friendly message, and you will usually get a reply.

Do you really want to fill up a whole day or an afternoon? Perhaps it is cold and rainy and you want to talk to someone. Then it is time to undertake a project that may turn out to be profitable and will also fill some spare time. Call the major cell phone companies to determine the best rate for your phone needs. This will pay off. Let's hope you end up with the cheapest rates, and that will mean money in your pocket for your day of cell phone rating.

Many people have gone out of their way to help you at this difficult time of your life. When you regain your composure, take them to lunch, perhaps several people at a time. This could even be a light picnic in the park, or maybe a continental breakfast at home. Be sure to repay all those people who were extremely caring with their actions. An extra show of caring to express your thanks will mean a great deal, and it might encourage them to continue asking you to do things with them. It may get them over their awkwardness with your new single status.

Starting to Socialize

Remember this in choosing friends: you need to be around positive-thinking people. Negative people will pull you down mentally. Talk to others who are in the same boat. Friends who have been widowed will willingly share experiences and suggestions with you. Attend a meeting of a support group. Ask those whom you have seen overcome adversity what helped them the most, but try to seek out those who have an upbeat attitude toward life.

It is likely to take a real effort on your part to make yourself get out and about. Do not wait too terribly long. Perhaps the way to re-initiate your social contacts is to go back to something you enjoyed previously, whether it is bridge or golf, or attending the theater or the symphony. Try to set up a small group of old or new friends to do these activities regularly. Then put on your make-up and a suitable outfit and sashay out with a smile to greet people.

If your church or synagogue has a singles' group, don't be afraid to go. Don't forget, we are all awkward about opening ourselves up to new relationships. Sometimes your bank or a travel agent will plan group tours for single people. Give it a try. Consider a cruise with single people of all ages on board.

Each widow and widower will decide when he or she is ready to date. Yes, the word "date" can become part of your vocabulary. Not the kind you eat, but the ritual of going out to dinner with an old friend or a new acquaintance. You will know when you are ready, if ever, to venture into a new dating period of life. If you have been exercising, eating right, keeping up with the paperwork, and associating with positive people, you will be interesting to others and ready for new episodes in your life.

In Conclusion

The only courage that matters is the kind
that gets you from one minute to the next.

You will find the courage to move forward with your life. After the death of a loved one, most of us start out living minute to minute. But this will grow into hours, days, weeks, and months; and then the first-year anniversary will arrive, and you will know that you have survived. You are now living another chapter of your own full book of life. You have found that you can be strong, you can make tough decisions, and you can sustain creativity and resourcefulness. Recognize how much you have to offer to yourself and to others.

Webster's definition of alone is "apart from anything or anyone else" or "without any other person." This description will fit some part of your life now. No matter how many children you have, no matter how much your friends help, and no matter how strong your faith is, basically you must face time alone. Remember that you do have the inner resources to face what has befallen you and to move toward happiness once more.

Corrine shares some personal thoughts with this original poem spelling an acronym about her personal journey:

Alone
W is for widowhood, which means you are a woman alone.
I is for an individual, which means you are a person standing alone.
D is for your spouse's death, which left you alone.
O is for others caring, but still leaving you alone.
W is for wishing, not to be left alone.
H is for happiness, which you will find on your own and alone.
O is for one, which is you alone.
O is for options you will have to choose alone.
D is for days and nights, you will live alone.

References

Bartlett, John. 1968. *Bartlett's Familiar Quotations*, 14th edition. Emily Morrison Beck, editor. Boston: Little, Brown, and Company.

Colgrove, Melba, Harold H. Bloomfield, and Peter McWilliams.1991. *How to Survive the Loss of a Love*, Los Angeles, CA: Prelude Press.

George, David L. (editor). 1952. *The Family Book of Best Loved Poems*, Garden City, NY: Doubleday & Company, Inc.

Guralnick, David B. (editor). 1982. *Webster's New World Dictionary of the American Language*, New York: New World Dictionaries/Simon and Schuster.

Martz, Sandra (editor). 1987. *When I Am an Old Woman I Shall Wear Purple*, Watsonville, CA: Papier Mache Press.

The Quotable Woman. 1991. Philadelphia, PA: Running Press.

About the Authors

Corrine Jacobson: Corrine lived in Fort Worth, Texas from the age of ten. She attended Texas Tech University, leaving to marry at an early age. Thirteen years later, when she found herself divorced with two young sons to provide for, she joined an industrial safety-equipment business. Although management in this field was unknown for women at that time, she became the president of a major distributorship, supervising three warehouses with thirty employees, calling on firms, and building a business with annual sales over $7 million. During this time, her second marriage brought her 22 years of happiness as she helped her spouse rear his three children in addition to her own. This phase of her life ended suddenly when she was widowed only a few years after her retirement. As someone who always sought solutions to the problems she faced, she looked for books on the realities and responsibilities of widowhood. She was only able to find books of quotations and books on grieving. Because she is a positive thinker, this book was written to help other widows find a new path in their lives.

Rose Rubin: Corrine is my friend, and I grieved with her when her beloved spouse died. I also realized that she was using her management and organization skills of a retired executive, as well as her inner strength and special people savvy, in handling the difficulties of being widowed. So, knowing how much she has helped others all her life, I urged her to write notes about what she had to do when she was widowed and how she went about it. The objective was to provide a useful record so others could benefit from her experiences and abilities, and our book emerged from her good records.

Rose M. Rubin, Ph.D., is Professor of Economics, Department of Economics, Fogelman College of Business and Economics, at the University of Memphis, Memphis, TN. She received her B.A. from Wellesley College, M.A. from Emory University, and Ph.D. from Kansas State University, all in economics. She has co-authored two books about American households, *Working Wives and Dual-Earner Families* (1994) and *Expenditures of Older Americans* (1997). She has also authored dozens of scholarly research papers on health and aging in refereed academic journals, such as: the *Journals of Gerontology, The Gerontologist, Medical Care, Social Science Quarterly, Monthly Labor*

Review, the Journal of Applied Gerontology, the Journal of Family and Economic Issues, and numerous other economics and social science journals.

Acknowledgements

We gratefully acknowledge those who have shared experiences with us or have offered valuable comments from reading the manuscript at various stages of development. The late Dr. Carolyn Shaw Bell, who was Catherine Cowan Professor of Economics Emeritus of Wellesley College, was most generous in providing helpful suggestions. Ms. Jane Schneider of Schneider Communications, Memphis, TN utilized our input and provided insights based on her direction of the series *The Age Adventure* for PBS, with Corrine and Rose featured in one segment. We thank writer Hollace Weiner for copy editing the manuscript, Alexa Kirk for cover design, and Caryn FitzGerald for shepherding the manuscript through to publication. We express our thanks to each of them, as they have improved upon our efforts and contributed to the usefulness you will derive from this book. We, of course, take full responsibility for the contents. This book does not provide legal advice or act as legal counsel in any manner.

CPSIA information can be obtained
at www.ICGtesting.com
Printed in the USA
BVOW08s1113141117
500389BV00001B/128/P